T0390247

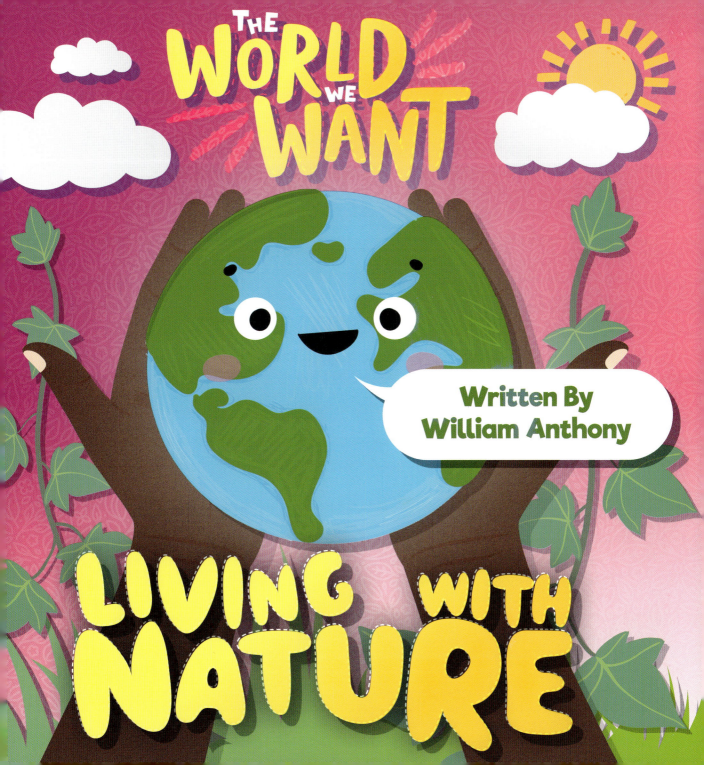

American adaptation copyright © 2026 by North Star Editions, Mendota Heights, MN 55120. All rights reserved. No part of this book may be reproduced or utilized in any form or by any means without written permission from the publisher.

Living with Nature © 2024 BookLife Publishing
This edition is published by arrangement with BookLife Publishing

sales@northstareditions.com
888-417-0195

Library of Congress Control Number:
The Library of Congress Control Number is available on the Library of Congress website.

ISBN
979-8-89359-335-8 (library bound)
979-8-89359-419-5 (paperback)

979-8-89359-389-1 (epub)
979-8-89359-365-5 (hosted ebook)

Printed in the United States of America
Mankato, MN
092025

Written by:
William Anthony

Edited by:
Rebecca Phillips-Bartlett

Designed by:
Rob Delph

All facts, statistics, web addresses and URLs in this book were verified as valid and accurate at time of writing. No responsibility for any changes to external websites or references can be accepted by either the author or publisher.

PHOTO CREDITS

All images are courtesy of Shutterstock.com, unless otherwise specified. Front Cover – Tanarch, cosmaa, Hafid Firman, GoodStudio, venimo, StockSmartStart. 4&5 – Jacob Lund, Photoongraphy. 6&7 – PARALAXIS, baldezh, 4 PM production. 8&9 – Amateur007, Graphic_Stocks, ToYoPHoTo, fokke baarssen, Todor Stoyanov-Raveo, Q88, Vitalii Stock, Bohdan Populov, Gilang Prihardono, Alexander Knyazhinsky. 10&11 – Victoria Nevzorova, Nikola Fific, Brian A Jackson. 12&13 – ivector, Igogosha, Alexxndr, Silentgunman, Vector Icon Systems. 14&15 – Jordi Jornet, Studio Light and Shade, Archi0780 – Own work, CC BY-SA 4.0, https://commons.wikimedia.org/w/index.php?curid=3083981. 16&17 – New Africa, Alexxndr, Kulinenko.G, Krys87, Kiattipong, ornavi. 18&19 – marilyn barbone, Parilov, bessyana. 20&21 – thebeststocker, Pixel-Shot, etorres, Elena Shashkina, Benjamin Scribe, keko64, 5PH, Oleksandr Derevianko, souga.biz. 22&23 – Adwo, Tapui, Spotmatik Ltd. Vectors throughout – Tanarch, cosmaa, Hafid Firman, GoodStudio, venimo, StockSmartStart.

CONTENTS

Page 4   No New Planet
Page 6   Daily Life
Page 8   Eco-Friendly Living
Page 10 Transportation
Page 14 Earth-Sheltered Homes
Page 18 Plant-Based Meals
Page 22 Love Our Planet
Page 24 Glossary and Index

Words that look like this can be found in the glossary on page 24.

NO NEW PLANET

We live on planet Earth. We share Earth with lots of animals and plants. Together, they all make up our planet's ecosystem.

YOU LIVE SOMEWHERE ON PLANET EARTH! CAN YOU SPOT WHERE?

We must look after our planet. We don't have a new planet to go to. We all need to work together with nature to take care of the environment.

DAILY LIFE

Everybody's daily life is different. What is a normal day like for you? How do you travel to school? What sort of home do you live in? What types of food do you eat?

Many of the things we do every day can cause problems for our planet. They can pollute our air, damage forests, and make Earth hotter than it should be.

ECO-FRIENDLY LIVING

We make choices every day. Your choices might be about what sandwich to eat or whether to take the bus or walk. Often, one of our options has a bigger impact on the planet than the other.

For example, we choose how we power our homes. We can choose to create power using coal or oil, which is bad for our planet. Or we can use wind or solar power, which is good for our planet.

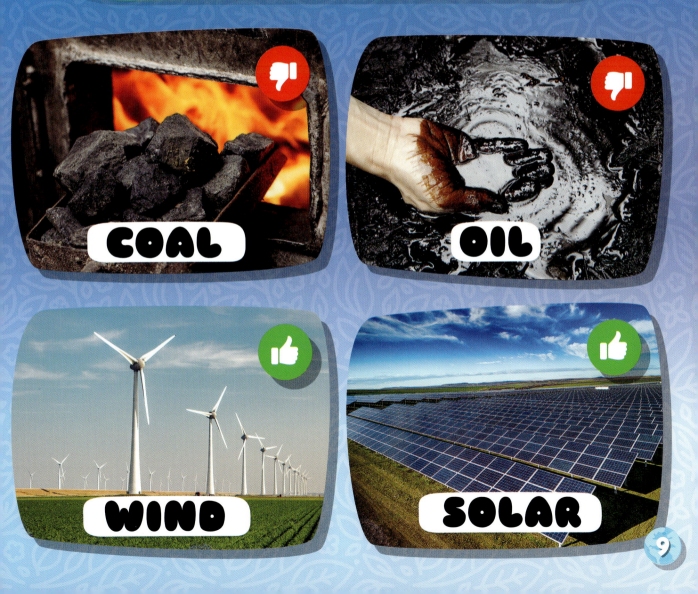

TRANSPORTATION

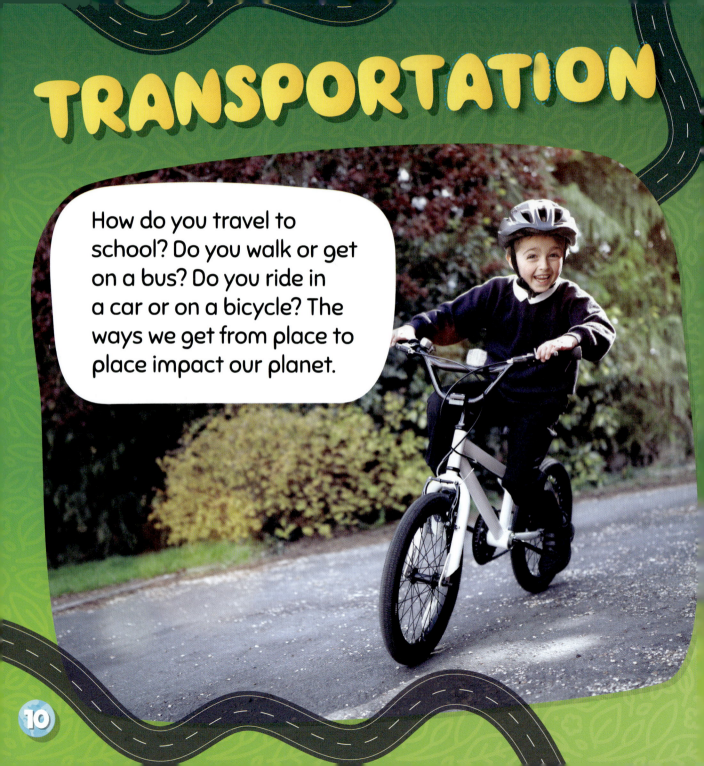

How do you travel to school? Do you walk or get on a bus? Do you ride in a car or on a bicycle? The ways we get from place to place impact our planet.

Many vehicles are powered by harmful oil. This includes cars and buses. When we choose to walk or ride a bicycle instead, we are choosing to help our planet.

Is it better for 30 people to use 30 cars or for 30 people to ride together on 1 bus?

3.

Week 1

Monday – Bus to school
Tuesday – Car to school
Wednesday – Car to school
Thursday – Bike to school
Friday – Bus to school
Saturday – Walk to town
Sunday – Car to shops

Underneath WEEK 1, keep a diary of every time you travel and how you do it. Live this week normally.

4.

Week 1

Monday – Bus to school
Tuesday – Car to school
 – school
 – ool
 –
 –

Week 2

Monday – Walk to school
Tuesday – Bike to school
Wednesday – Walk to school
Thursday – Bike to school
Friday – Bus to school
Saturday – Bike to town
Sunday – Bus to shops

For WEEK 2, try to make some changes. Can you change that car journey to a bicycle ride? Can you swap a bus ride for a walk?

EARTH-SHELTERED HOMES

What type of home do you live in? Do you live in a house with a yard or an apartment in a town? Some people live close to nature in earth-sheltered homes.

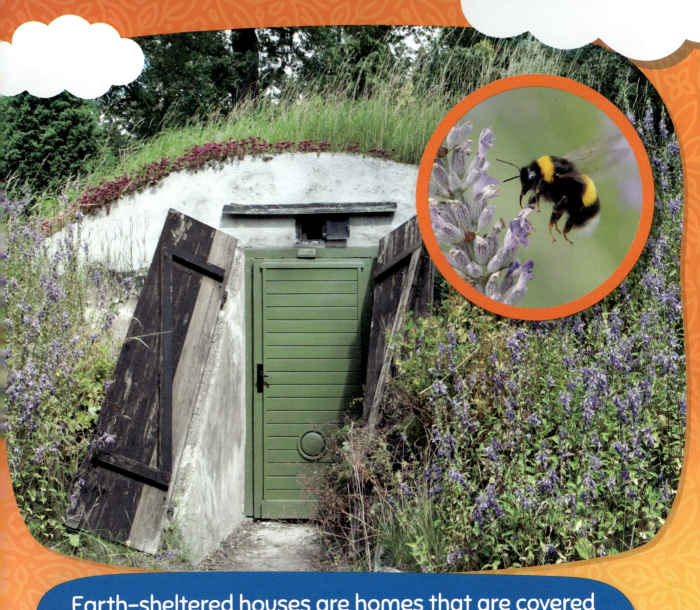

Earth-sheltered houses are homes that are covered by soil and plants. This helps to keep the homes warm without needing extra power. The plants and grass on top of the house are great for wildlife such as bees.

PLANT-BASED MEALS

What is your favorite meal? There are a few different types of food that people can eat. Some <u>diets</u> include meat. Others are meat-free or only include things made from plants.

Different diets impact our planet in different ways. Farming animals uses lots of land for animals to live on and grow their food on. This means we often cut down trees to make space for them.

Cutting down trees is not good for our planet.

LOVE OUR PLANET

Do you have any new ideas for how to keep Earth healthy?

Earth needs our help to keep it healthy. The choices we make every day help us to look after our planet. People have found lots of smart ways to help us live with nature.

Whether it is your transportation choices, earth-sheltered housing, or eating plant-based food, you can help to create the world we all want!

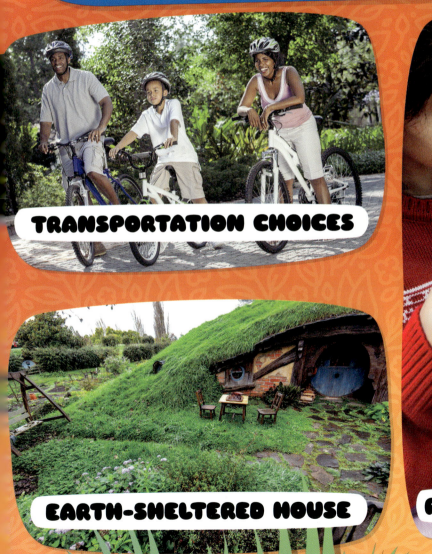

TRANSPORTATION CHOICES

EARTH-SHELTERED HOUSE

PLANT-BASED DIET

GLOSSARY

DESIGN	plan and then make something
DIETS	the types of food that a person or animal usually eats
ECOSYSTEM	everything that lives together in an environment
ENVIRONMENT	the surroundings that an animal, plant, or human lives in
NATURE	the world around us and everything in it that is not made by humans
POLLUTE	to make land, water, or air dirty and unsafe
SOLAR POWER	energy from the sun
VEHICLES	machines that are used to carry people or things from one place to another
WILDLIFE	animals that live in natural places

INDEX

air	7	**meat**	18	**schools**	6, 10
animals	4, 19	**plants**	4, 15, 17–18, 20, 23	**trees**	19
food	6, 18–19, 23				
homes	6, 9, 14–15	**power**	9, 15		